Broadway

Arranged by Dan Coates

CONTENTS

Cover photograph:
New York Skyline © istockphoto.com/adamkaz

ISBN-10: 0-7390-6003-1
ISBN-13: 978-0-7390-6003-2

AND ALL THAT JAZZ

Lyrics by Fred Ebb
Music by John Kander
Arranged by Dan Coates

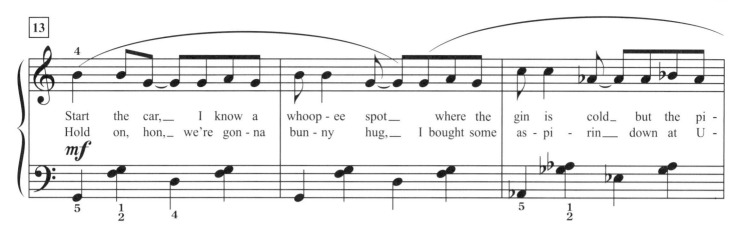

Start the car,__ I know a whoop - ee spot__ where the gin is cold__ but the pi -
Hold on, hon,__ we're gon - na bun - ny hug,__ I bought some as - pi - rin__ down at U -

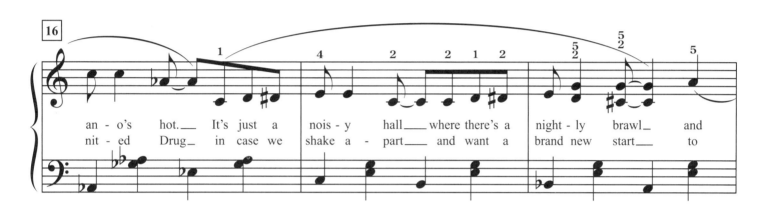

an - o's hot.__ It's just a nois - y hall__ where there's a night - ly brawl__ and
nit - ed Drug__ in case we shake a - part__ and want a brand new start__ to

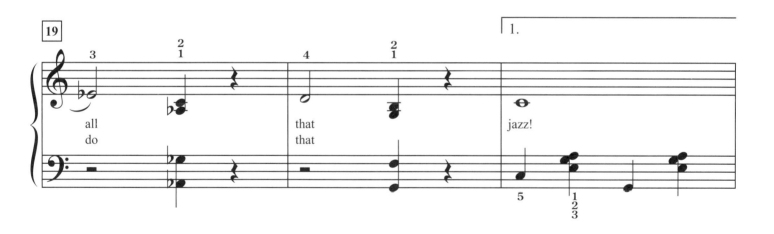

all
do

that
that

jazz!

1.

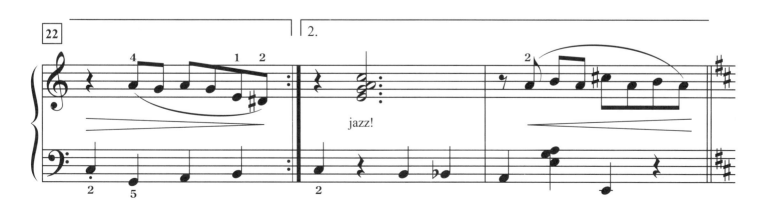

2.

jazz!

Oh, I'm gon-na see my She-ba shim-my shake.— (And

all that jazz!)— Oh, she's gon-na shim-my 'til her

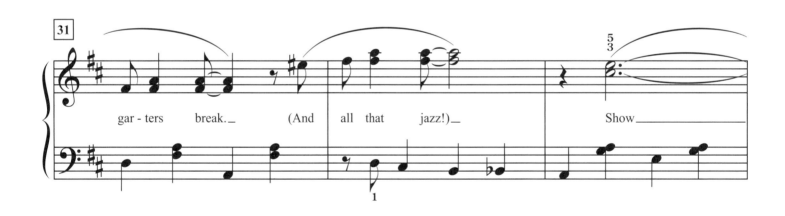

gar-ters break.— (And all that jazz!)— Show_____

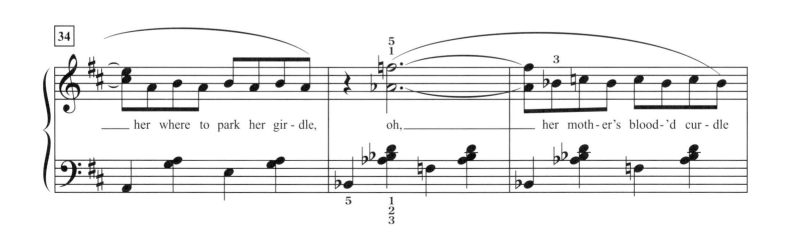

_____ her where to park her gir-dle, oh,_____ her moth-er's blood-'d cur-dle

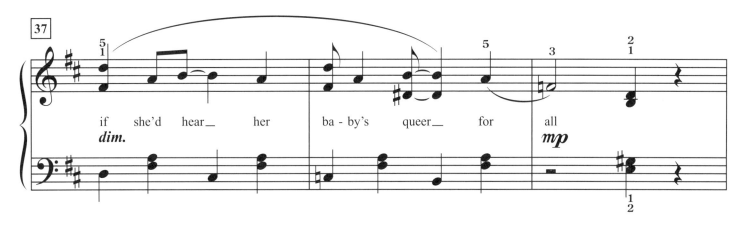

if she'd hear__ her ba - by's queer__ for all

that jazz!

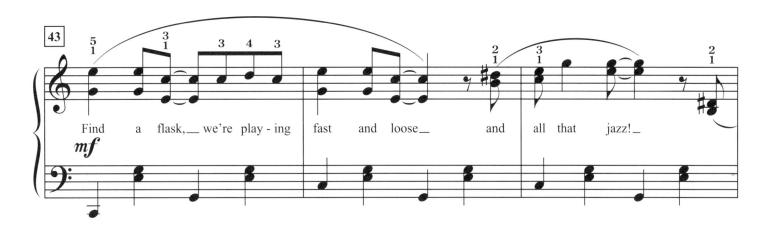

Find a flask,__ we're play - ing fast and loose__ and all that jazz!__

Right up here__ is where I store the juice,__ and

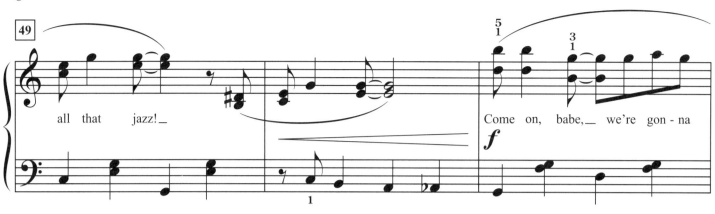

all that jazz!— Come on, babe,— we're gon-na

brush the sky.— I bet-cha Luck-y Lin - dy nev - er flew so high,— 'cause in the

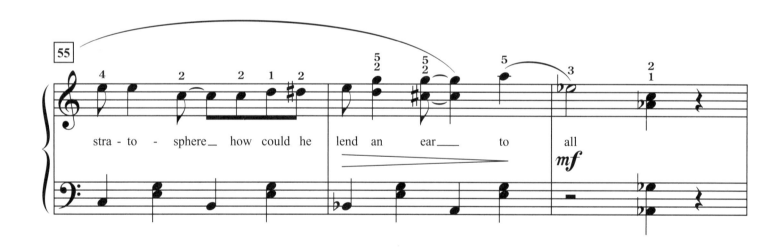

stra - to - sphere— how could he lend an ear— to all

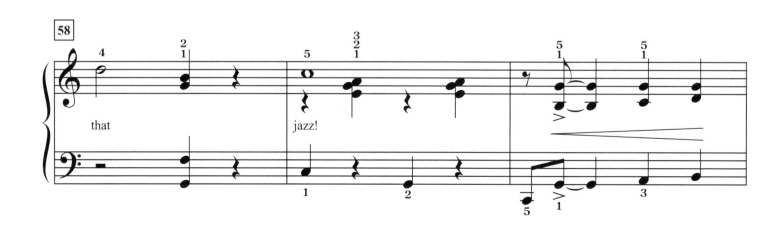

that jazz!

No, I'm no one's wife,__ but oh, I

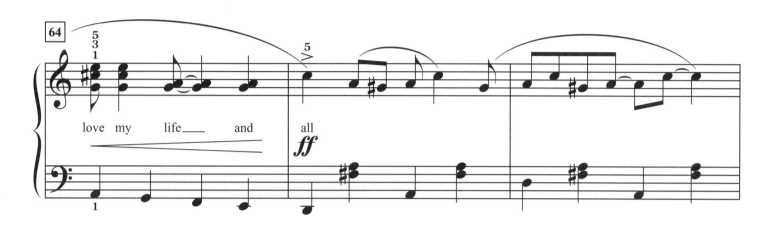

love my life__ and all

that jazz!

That jazz!

DANCING QUEEN

Words and Music by Benny Andersson,
Stig Anderson and Bjorn Ulvaeus
Arranged by Dan Coates

Bright disco beat, in two

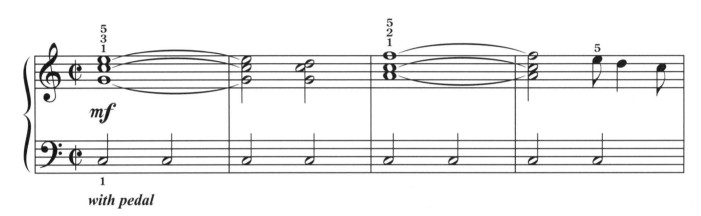

with pedal

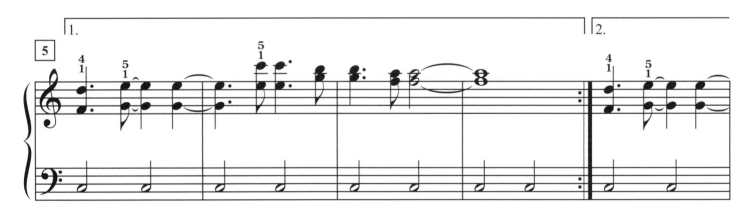

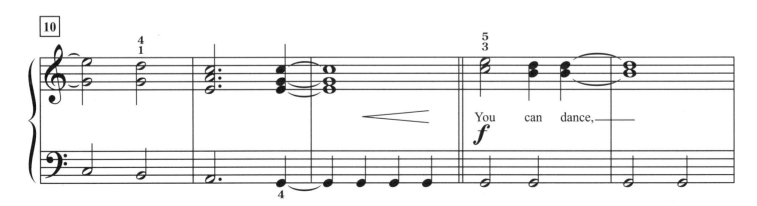

You can dance,

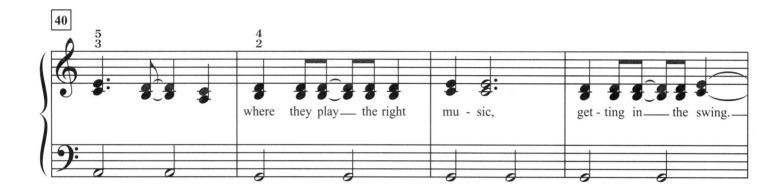

where they play — the right mu - sic, get - ting in — the swing.

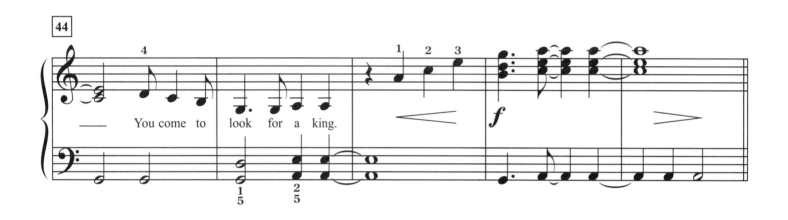

— You come to look for a king.

2. An - y - bod - y can be that guy.
3. You're a teas - er, you turn 'em on.

Night is young — and the mu - sic's high.
Leave 'em burn - in' and then you're gone.

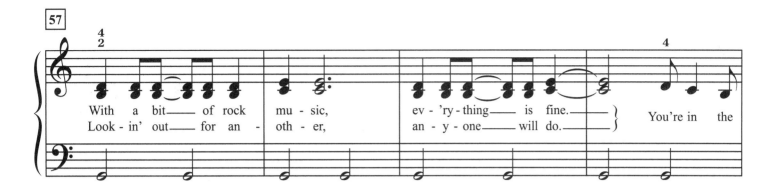

With a bit——— of rock mu - sic, ev - 'ry-thing——— is fine.——— You're in the
Look - in' out——— for an - oth - er, an - y - one——— will do.———

mood for a dance. And when——— you get a——— chance...
cresc.

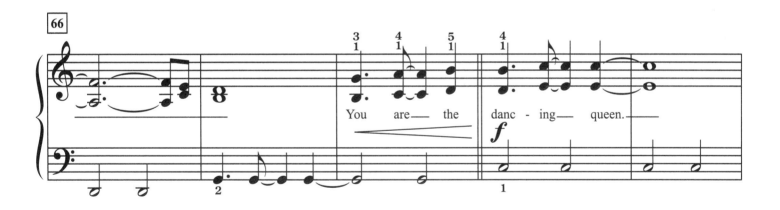

You are——— the danc - ing——— queen.———
f

Young and——— sweet,——— on - ly sev - en - teen.———

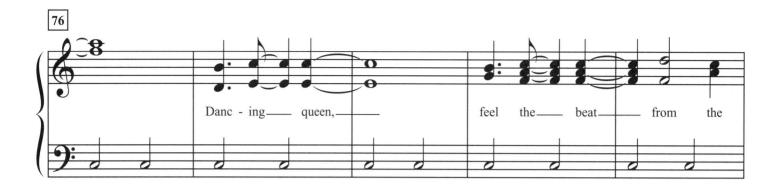

Danc - ing— queen,—— feel the— beat— from the

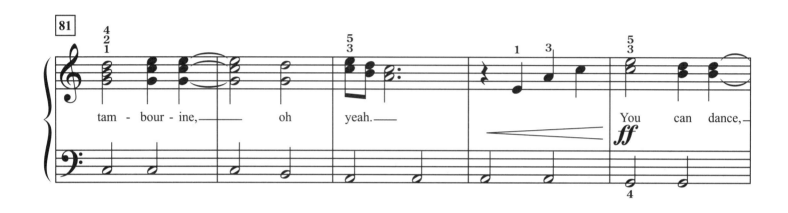

tam - bour - ine,— oh yeah.— You can dance,

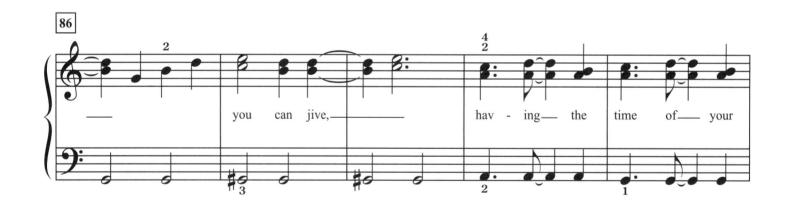

— you can jive,— hav - ing— the time of— your

life.— Ooh,— see that— girl,— watch that— scene,

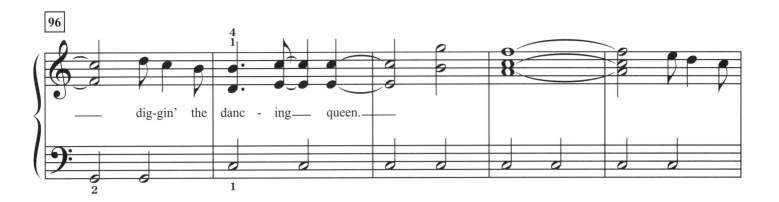

diggin' the danc - ing queen.

1. 2.

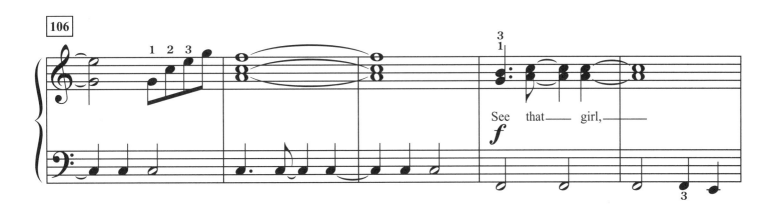

See that girl,

watch that scene, diggin' the danc - ing queen.

CAN YOU FEEL THE LOVE TONIGHT

from Walt Disney's *The Lion King*

Music by Elton John
Words by Tim Rice
Arranged by Dan Coates

Moderately slow ballad

1. There's a calm__ sur - ren - der to the rush__ of day,
2. There's a time__ for ev - 'ry - one if they on - ly learn

when the heat__ of the roll - ing world can be turned a - way.
that the twist - ing ka - lei - do - scope moves us all in__ turn.

An en - chant - ed mo - ment, and it sees__ me through.
There's a rhyme__ and rea - son to the wild__ out - doors

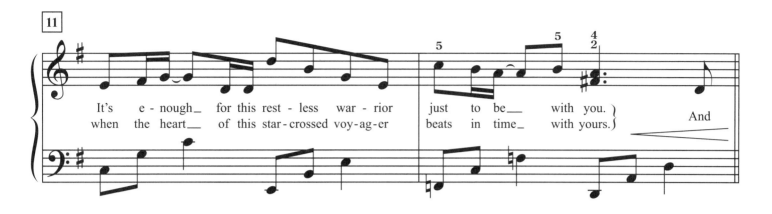

It's e - nough_ for this rest - less war - rior just to be_ with you.
when the heart_ of this star - crossed voy - ag - er beats in time_ with yours.
And

can you feel_ the love_ to - night?_ It is where we are._

mf

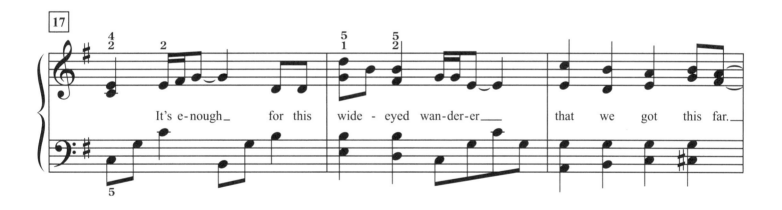

It's e - nough_ for this wide - eyed wan - der - er_ that we got this far._

_ And can you feel_ the love_ to - night,

how it's laid to rest?___ It's e-nough___ to make

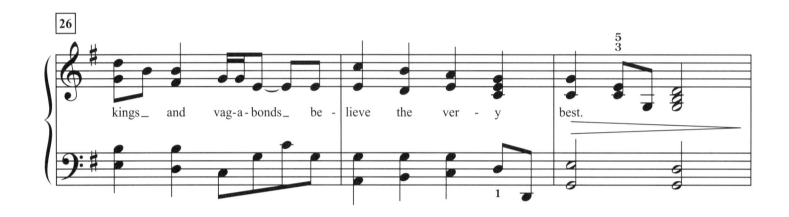

kings___ and vag-a-bonds___ be- lieve the ver - y best.

1.

2.

It's e-nough___ to make kings___ and vag-a-bonds___ be- lieve the ver - y best.

rit. e dim.

EASE ON DOWN THE ROAD

Words and Music by Charlie Smalls
Arranged by Dan Coates

Moderately fast

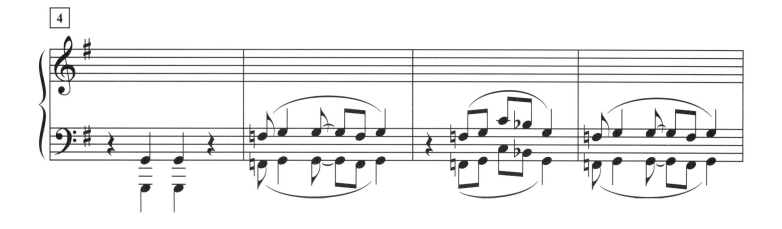

Come on and   ease on___ down,   ease on down___ the road.

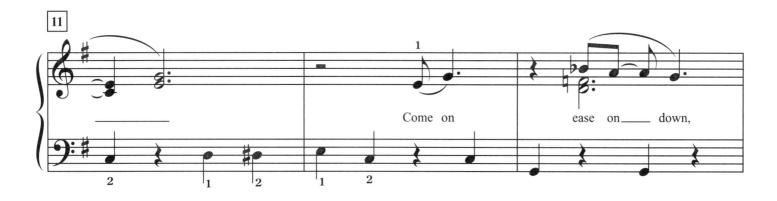

Come on ease on___ down,

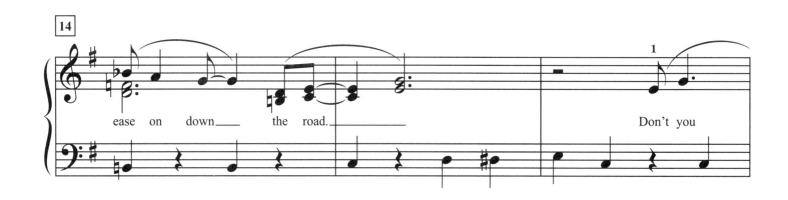

ease on down___ the road.___ Don't you

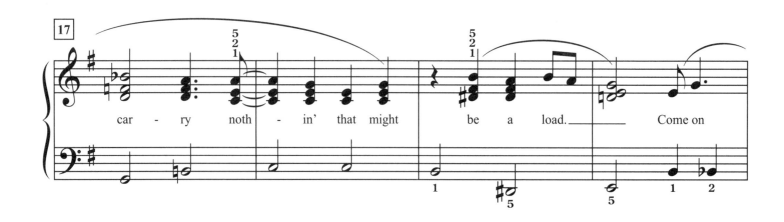

car - ry noth - in' that might be a load.___ Come on

ease on down,___ ease on___ down, down the road.

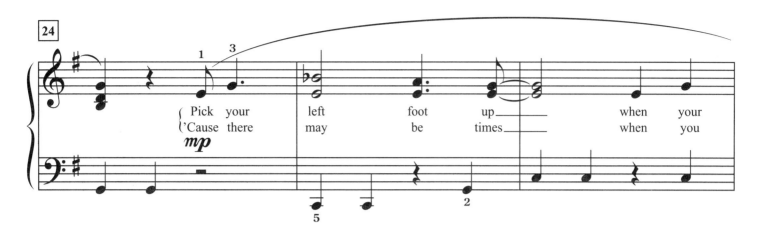

Pick your left foot up_____ when your
'Cause there may be times_____ when you

mp

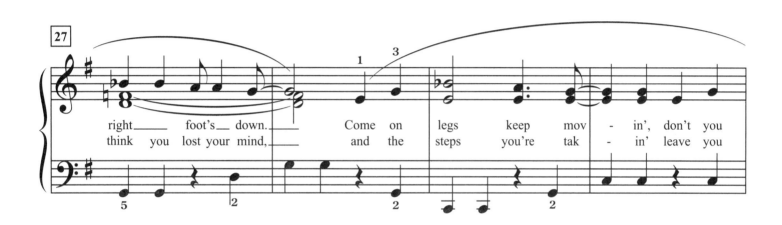

right_____ foot's_____ down._____ Come on legs keep mov - in', don't you
think you lost your mind,_____ and the steps you're tak - in' leave you

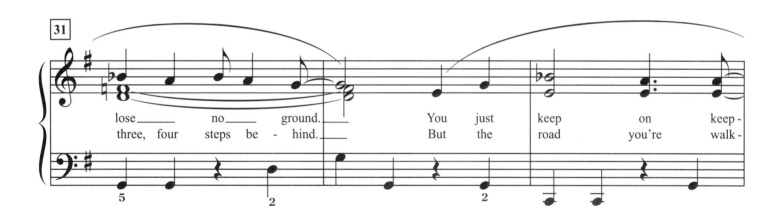

lose_____ no_____ ground._____ You just keep on keep -
three, four steps be - hind._____ But the road you're walk -

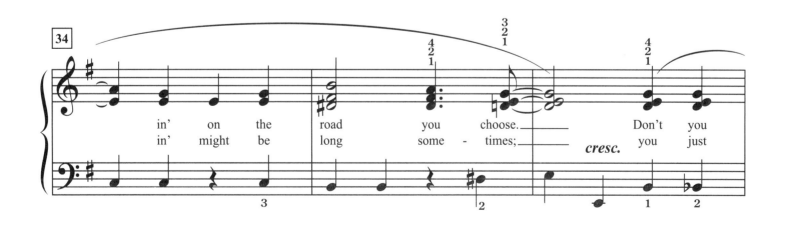

in' on the road you choose._____ Don't you
in' might be long some - times;_____ you just

cresc.

give up   up   walk-in' 'cause you   gave___ up   shoes,   no.___
keep   on   truck-in' and you'll   be___ just   fine,   yeah.___

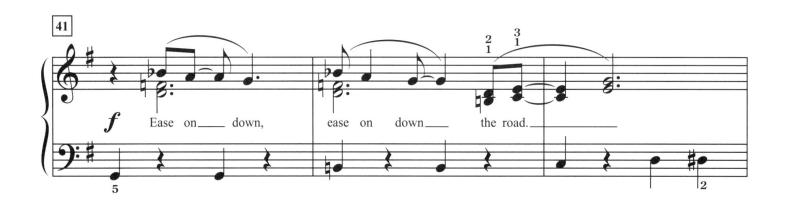

f   Ease on___ down,   ease on down___ the road.___

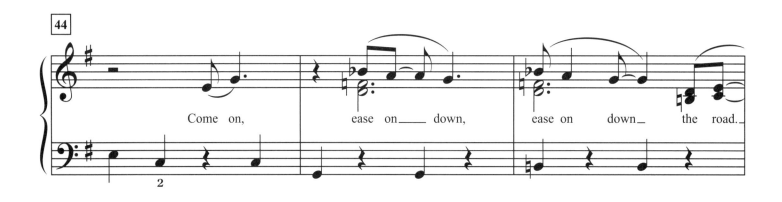

Come on,   ease on___ down,   ease on down___ the road.

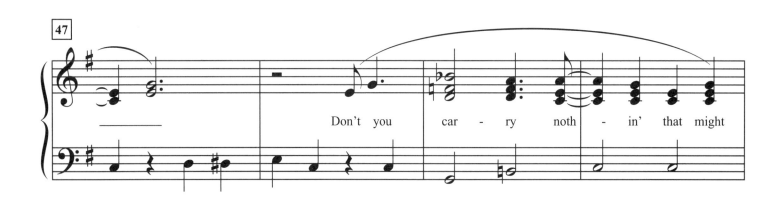

___   Don't you   car - ry   noth - in' that might

be a load._____ Come on

ease on down,_____ ease on_____

_____ down, down the...

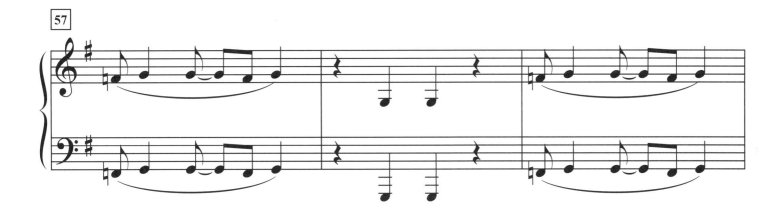

sfz

HOLD ME, THRILL ME, KISS ME

Words and Music by Harry Noble
Arranged by Dan Coates

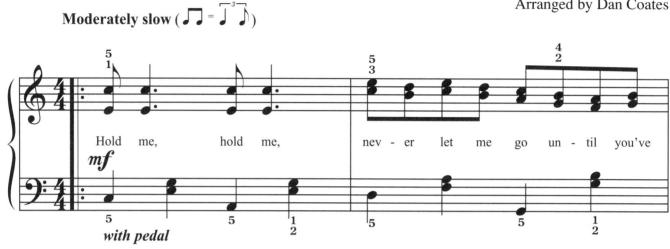

Thrill me, thrill me, walk me down the lane where shad-ows will be, will be

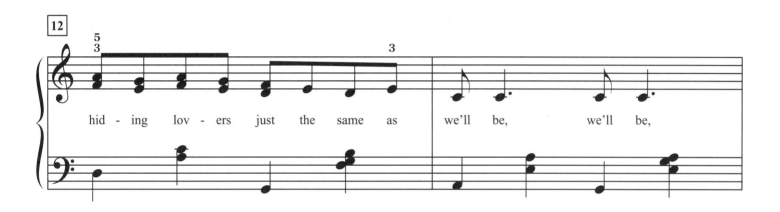

hid-ing lov-ers just the same as we'll be, we'll be,

when you make me tell you I love you. They

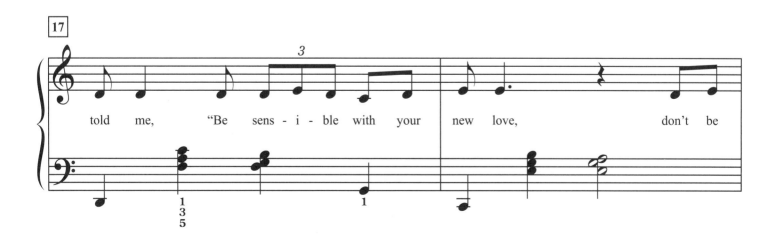

told me, "Be sens-i-ble with your new love, don't be

fooled think - ing this is the last you'll find." But

they nev - er stood in the dark with you, love,——————— when you

take me in your arms and drive me slow - ly out of my mind.

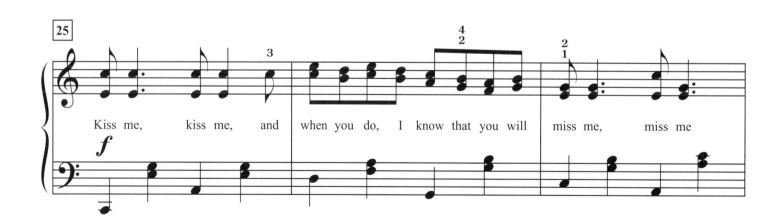

Kiss me, kiss me, and when you do, I know that you will miss me, miss me

if we ev-er say a-dieu, so   kiss me,   kiss me,   make me tell you I'm in love with

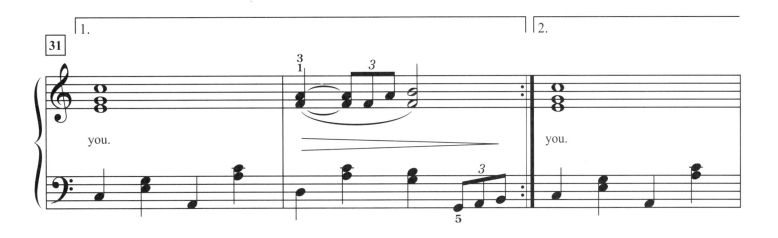

1.   2.

you.   you.

Nev-er, nev-er, nev-er let me   go.   Nev-er, nev-er, nev-er let me

go.   *molto rit.*   *mp*

HOW LUCKY YOU ARE

Words and Music by
Stephen Flaherty and Lynn Ahrens
Arranged by Dan Coates

When the news is all bad,— when you're sour— and blue,— when you

start to get mad,— you should do—— what I do:

Tell your - self　how luck - y you are.___　When your

life's go - ing wrong,___　when the fates are un - kind,___　when you're limp - ing a - long___　and get kicked

___ from be - hind,　tell your - self　how luck - y you are.

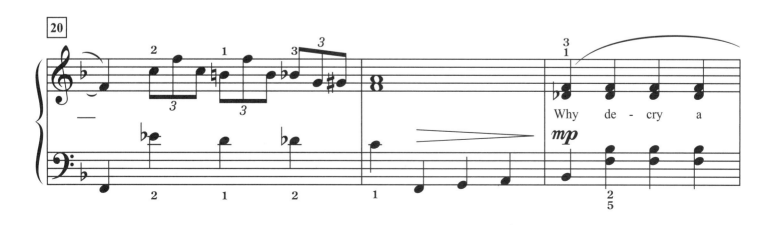

___　Why de - cry a

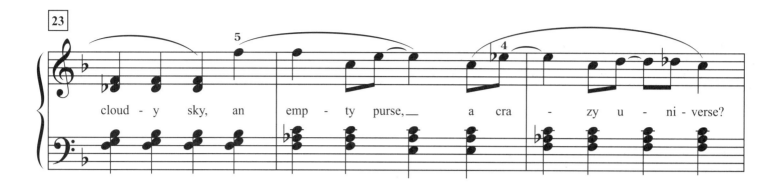

cloud - y sky, an emp - ty purse,__ a cra - zy u - ni - verse?

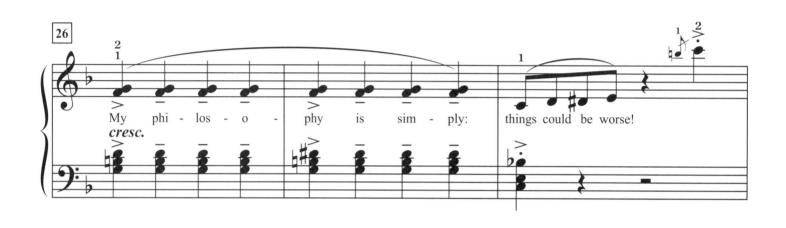

My phi - los - o - phy is sim - ply: things could be worse!

cresc.

So be hap - py you're here.__ Think of life as a thrill!__ And if

f

worse comes to worse_ (as we all__ know it will), thank your luck - y star_

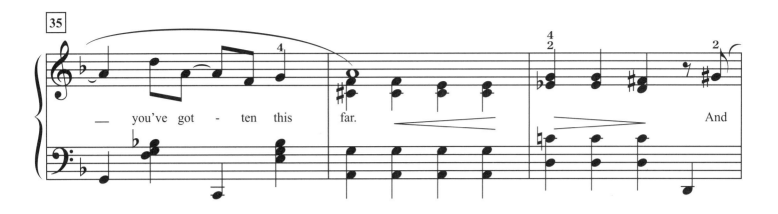

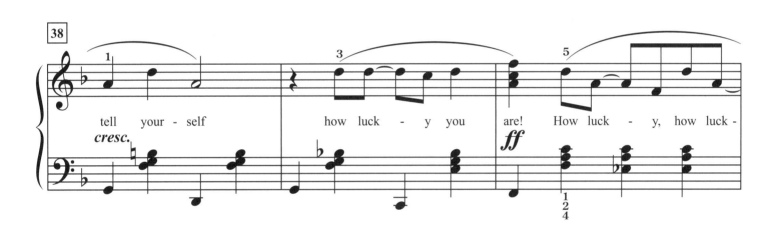

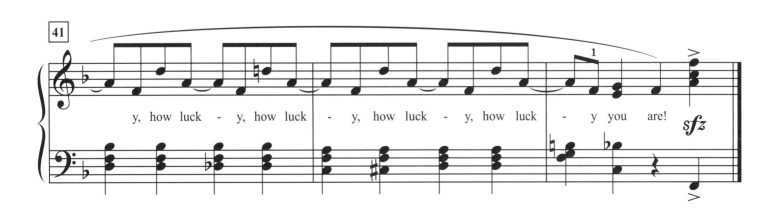

MAKE THEM HEAR YOU

Lyrics by Lynn Ahrens
Music by Stephen Flaherty
Arranged by Dan Coates

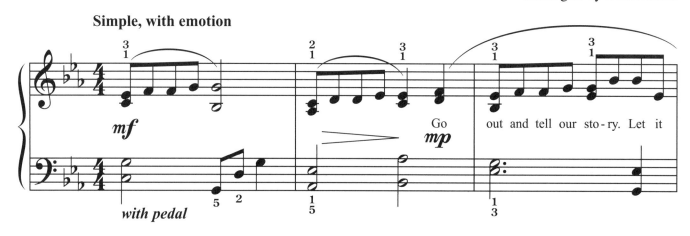

hear you. And say to those who blame us for the way we chose to fight that

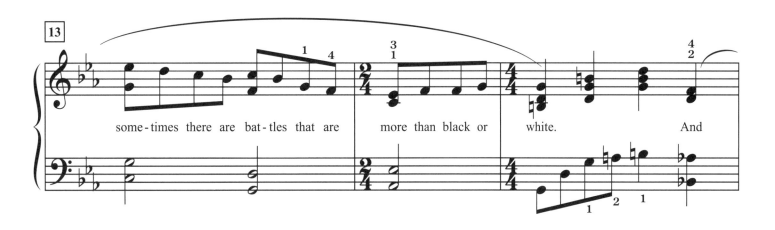

some-times there are bat-tles that are more than black or white. And

I could not put down my sword when jus-tice was my right. Make them hear you. Make them

hear you. Go out and tell the sto-ry to your

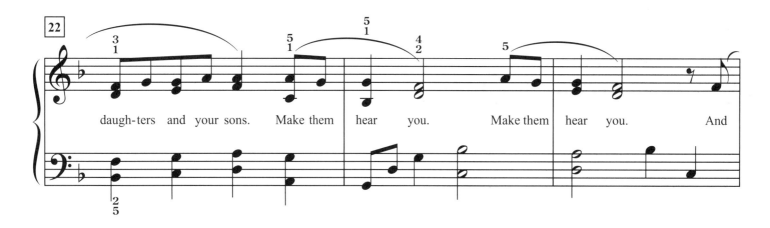

daugh-ters and your sons. Make them hear you. Make them hear you. And

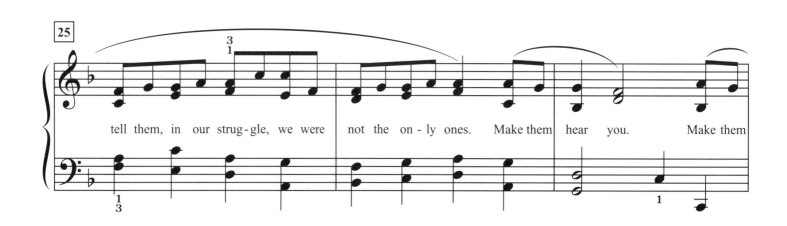

tell them, in our strug-gle, we were not the on-ly ones. Make them hear you. Make them

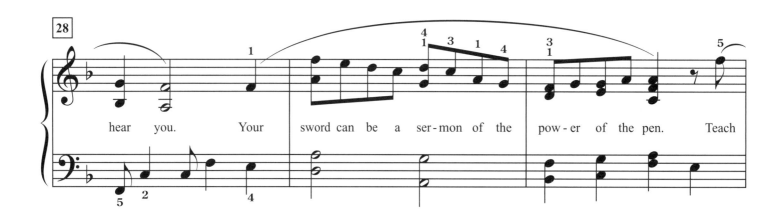

hear you. Your sword can be a ser-mon of the pow-er of the pen. Teach

ev-'ry child to raise his voice and then, my bro-thers, then will

rall.

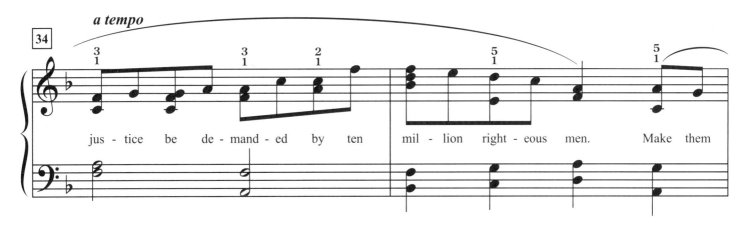

jus - tice be de - mand - ed by ten mil - lion right - eous men. Make them

hear you. When they hear you, I'll be near you a -

gain.

ON THE STREET WHERE YOU LIVE

Lyrics by Alan Jay Lerner
Music by Frederick Loewe
Arranged by Dan Coates

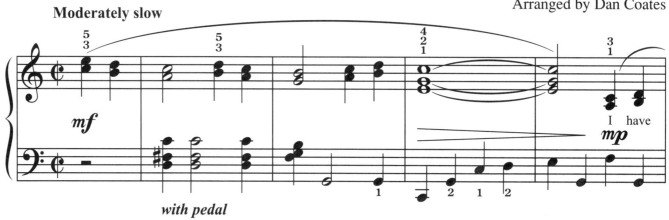

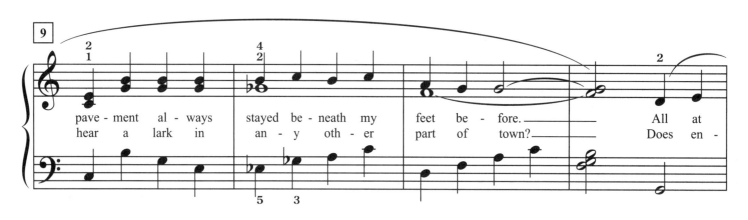

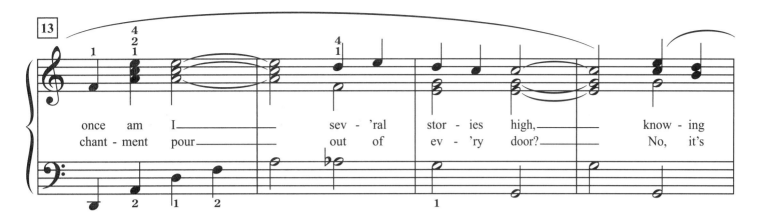

once am I_____ sev - 'ral stor - ies high, _____ know - ing
chant - ment pour _____ out of ev - 'ry door? _____ No, it's

I'm on the street where you live. _____ Are there
just on the

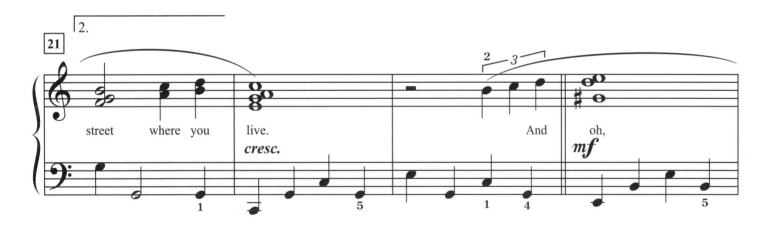

street where you live. And oh,
cresc. *mf*

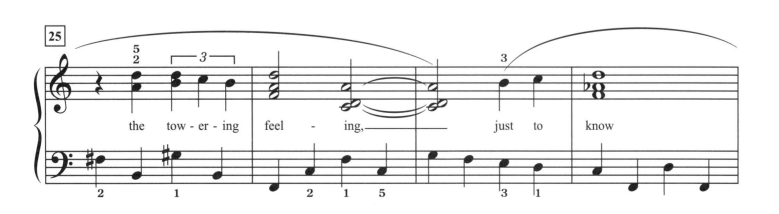

the tow - er - ing feel - ing, _____ just to know

some - how you are near! *dim.* The o -

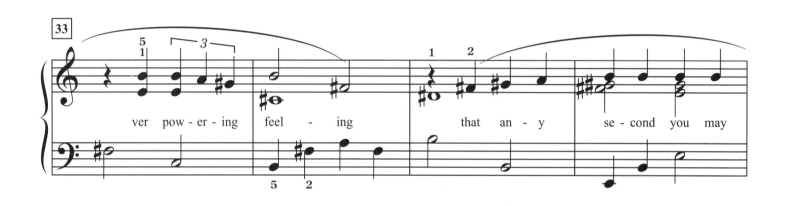

ver pow - er - ing feel - ing that an - y se - cond you may

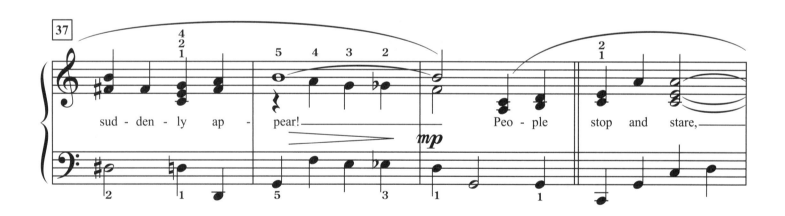

sud - den - ly ap - pear! *mp* Peo - ple stop and stare,

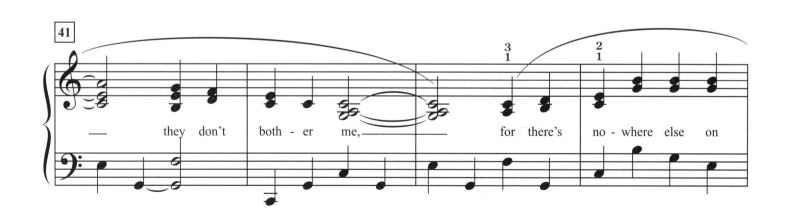

they don't both - er me, for there's no - where else on

earth that I would rath - er be._____ Let the time go by,_____

cresc. *mf*

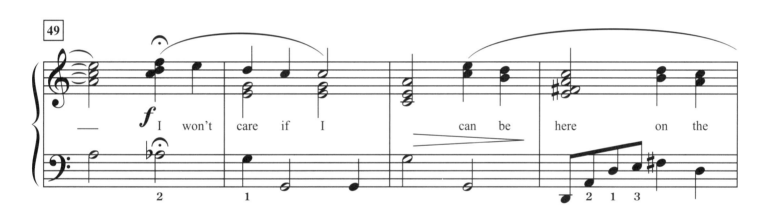

____ *f* I won't care if I can be here on the

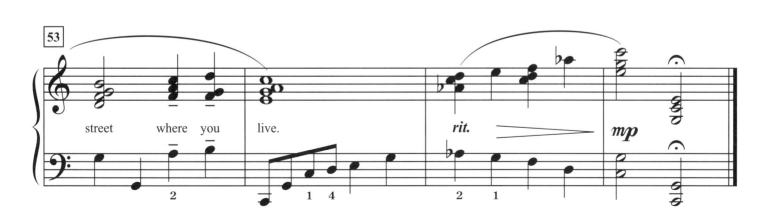

street where you live. *rit.* *mp*

TOGETHER WHEREVER WE GO

Lyrics by Stephen Sondheim
Music by Jule Styne
Arranged by Dan Coates

Brightly, in two

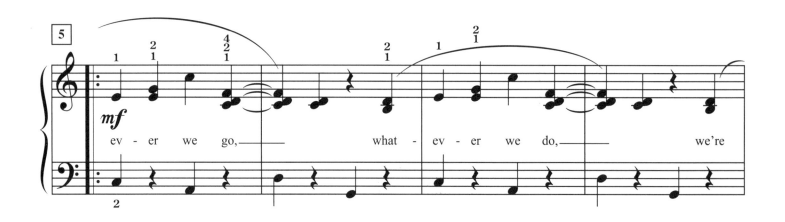

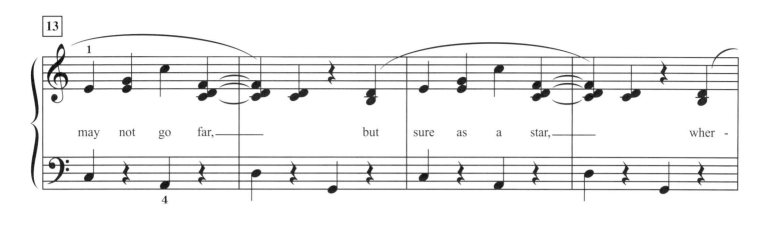

may not go far,_____ but sure as a star,_____ wher -

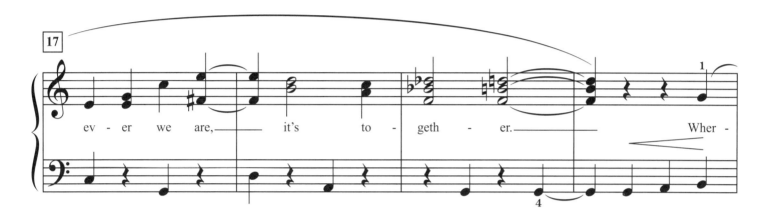

ev - er we are,_____ it's to - geth - er._____ Wher -

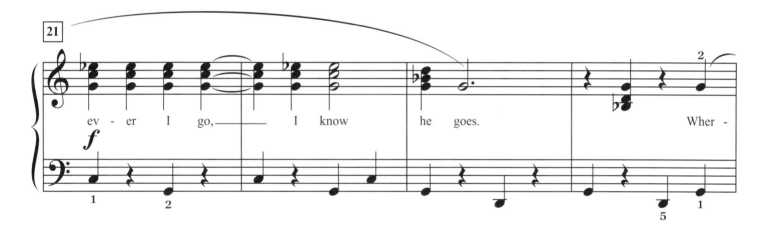

ev - er I go,_____ I know he goes. Wher -

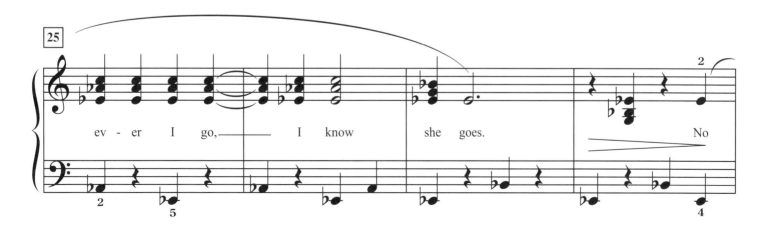

ev - er I go,_____ I know she goes. No

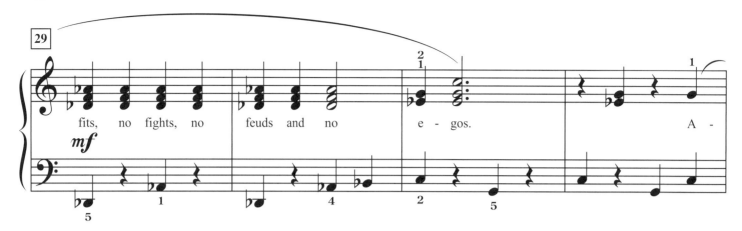

fits, no fights, no feuds and no e - gos. A -

mi - gos, to - geth - er! Through

thick and through thin, all out or all in, and

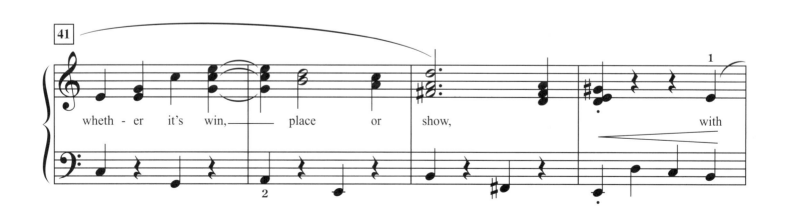

wheth - er it's win, place or show, with

you for me and me for you, we'll mud - dle through what - ev - er we do to -

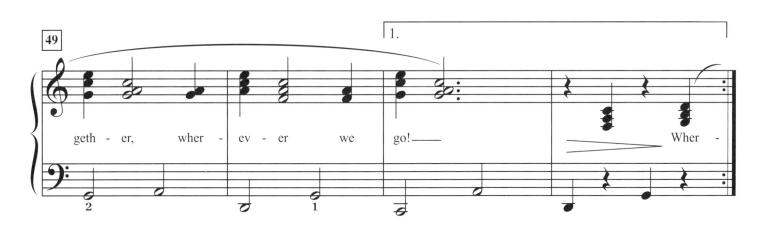

geth - er, wher - ev - er we go! Wher -

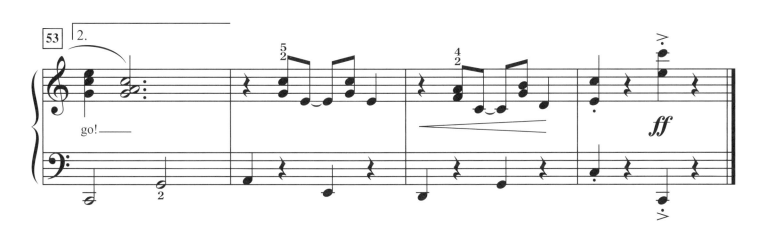

go!

HOW COULD I EVER KNOW

Lyrics by Marsha Norman
Music by Lucy Simon
Arranged by Dan Coates